THIS WALKER BOOK BELONGS TO:

Consultant Gussie Hearsey
On behalf of the Pre-school Playgroups Association

First published 1987 by Walker Books Ltd
87 Vauxhall Walk, London SE11 5HJ

This edition published 1992

© 1987 Colin West

Printed and bound in Hong Kong by
Dai Nippon Printing Co. Ltd

British Library Cataloguing in Publication Data
A catalogue record for this book is
available from the British Library.
ISBN 0-7445-2344-3

Ten Little Crocodiles

Colin West

WALKER BOOKS
LONDON

10

Ten little crocodiles
Sitting down to dine,

One of them ate too much pud,
And then there were…

Nine little crocodiles
Trying to lose weight,

One of them tried till he dropped,
And then there were...

Eight little crocodiles
Who hoped to go to heaven,

One of them went right away,
And then there were…

Seven little crocodiles
Doing magic tricks,

One of them went up in smoke,
And then there were…

Six little crocodiles
Learning how to drive,

One of them drove up a tree,
And then there were...

Five little crocodiles
Sailing to the shore,

One of them fell overboard,
And then there were...

Four little crocodiles
Going off to ski,

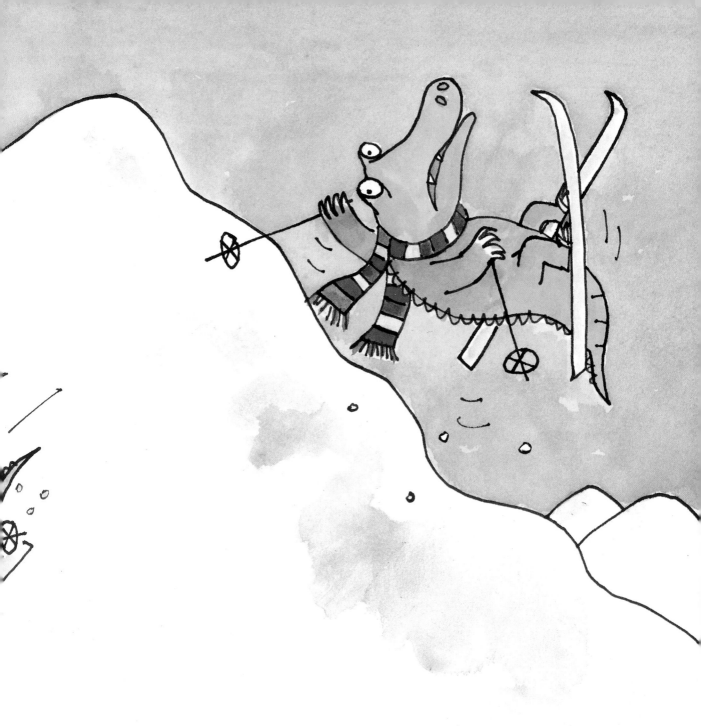

One of them turned somersaults,
And then there were…

Three little crocodiles
Visiting the zoo,

One of them got left behind,
And then there were…

2

Two little crocodiles
Sitting in the sun,

One of them went home to tea,
And then there was...

One little crocodile
Missing all his friends,

Let's have another look at them
Before the story ends…

One little crocodile
Then gets a big surprise…

All his friends are safe and sound,
He can't believe his eyes!

MORE WALKER PAPERBACKS
For You to Enjoy

Also by Colin West

ONE LITTLE ELEPHANT

Elephants sing and surf, skip and skate, jive and juggle in this most entertaining
counting-up rhyme – from one to ten – which proves that learning
can be a jumbo lot of fun!

0-7445-2345-1   £2.99

JUNGLE TALES

Five colourful cumulative stories, each with a twist in the tail.
Ideal for early readers.

0-7445-1065-1   *"Have you seen the crocodile?"*   £3.99
0-7445-1227-1   *"Hello, great big bullfrog!"*   £2.99
0-7445-1228-X   *"Not me," said the monkey*   £3.99
0-7445-1229-8   *"Pardon?" said the giraffe*   £3.99
0-7445-1785-0   *Go Tell It to the Toucan*   £3.99

I BOUGHT MY LOVE A TABBY CAT

Have you ever seen a tabby cat in a velvet hat, or a big fat pig in a
fancy wig, or an old grey goose in dainty shoes? These are just a few of the
extraordinary guests at a wedding, where the animals are better dressed than the bride!

"A nonsense rhyme that compares with Edward Lear at his best …
fitting and very funny illustrations." *Parents*

0-7445-2348-6   £3.99

**Walker Paperbacks are available from most booksellers, or by post from
Walker Books Ltd, PO Box 11, Falmouth, Cornwall TR10 9EN.**

To order, send: title, author, ISBN number and price for each book ordered, your full name and address
and a cheque or postal order for the total amount, plus postage and packing:

UK and BFPO Customers – £1.00 for first book, plus 50p for the second book and plus 30p for each additional book to a maximum charge of £3.00.
Overseas and Eire Customers – £2.00 for first book, plus £1.00 for the second book and plus 50p per copy for each additional book.
Prices are correct at time of going to press, but are subject to change without notice.